Woodcarving

designs

materials

technique

Walter Sack

VNR VAN NOSTRAND REINHOLD COMPANY
New York   Cincinnati   Toronto   London   Melbourne

Van Nostrand Reinhold Company
Regional Offices: New York
Cincinnati Chicago Millbrae Dallas
Van Nostrand Company International Offices:
London Toronto Melbourne

This book was originally
published in German under the
title *Holzschnitzen* by
Otto Maier Verlag Ravensburg
W. Germany.

Copyright © for *Holzschnitzen*
Otto Maier Verlag Ravensburg
1972. English Translation ©
Van Nostrand Reinhold Company
Ltd. 1973

Library of Congress Catolog Card
Number 72–1255 1
ISBN 0 442 29984 2 cl
ISBN 0 442 29982 6 pb

Translated from the German
by Frank Bradley
Photography – Walter Sack
and Barbara Schulten.
This book is printed in Univers
and is printed and bound in
Great Britain by Jolly & Barber Ltd., Rugby.

Published by Van Nostrand
Reinhold Inc.
450 West 33rd St., New York,
N.Y. 10001 and Van Nostrand
Reinhold Company Ltd.,
Molly Millars Lane,
Wokingham, Berkshire

Published simultaneously in
Canada by Van Nostrand
Reinhold Company Ltd.

16   15   14   13   12   11   10   9   8   7   6   5   4   3

Contents

Introduction

Wood has always been one of man's most popular raw materials, and carving is one of the oldest arts and crafts. Carvings of bone, horn and ivory have been preserved from Stone Age times, many of them real miniature works of art. Innumerable implements, tools and weapons must likewise have been made of wood, and perhaps ornamentally carved. Wood was probably the most abundant raw material and could easily be worked with flint scrapers and knives. But it is also relatively perishable and because of this a whole wealth of historical evidence has been lost to us for ever.

Modern tools are made of high quality steel, but carving remains an absorbing and undemanding hobby. All you need for it are your hands, a few tools and some wood. A small working space by a well-lit window is sufficient, and if the weather is fine you can carve in the open air.

Pure hand carving does not require a mallet; the carving tool is driven into the wood by hand pressure alone, and since this technique makes very little noise, it is particularly suitable for those who have to consider their neighbours or family.

You can work on a small wooden board placed on a table, with a layer of felt, cardboard or newspaper underneath to protect the table top. An old mat or a large sheet of wrapping paper can be laid under the table to protect the floor or carpet from the wood shavings which will be produced.

Sources of suitable wood

The tree is turned into timber

In the sawmill, the trunk is cut into sections; this is what the wood sculptor mainly uses. Thick boards are also called planks (see Fig. 1).

Most enterprises dealing with wood, such as joiners' and carpenters' workshops, cabinet makers and do-it-yourself shops will have scrap wood suitable for small carvings. Alternatively, you may be able to find a tree which has been felled by the roadside. If you keep your eyes open, you can often obtain suitable branches and trunk sections for very little money. Forestry authorities, private owners of woods, and above all sawmills and timber merchants are always good sources of supply. The latter also sell single boards and planks. There is no need to go to the expense of buying a whole trunk.

It is advisable to test the wood at the supplier's, particularly to see if it cuts well across the grain. The cut surface must not tear or be brittle; if it does, reject it and try another piece. Take a gouge along for wood sampling, but do keep it in a leather sheath.

Clearing out attics can produce much good and seasoned wood which might otherwise be burned. The boards of an old wooden cupboard can be used for low relief carvings. Oak beams obtained during demolition work can be valuable and cheap; stacks of firewood, too, can yield material for carving.

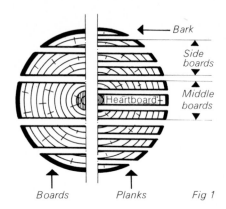

Fig 1

Bark

Side boards

Middle boards

Heartboard

Boards   *Planks*

During seasoning, boards and planks change in shape. They become concave on the left, and convex on the right (see Fig. 2). The reason for this is that the larger cells on the left evaporate more moisture. Hollowness therefore increases in the direction of the slab (Arrow 1). Towards the sapwood the boards become thinner, they shrink (Arrow 2). The heart board becomes convex on both sides.

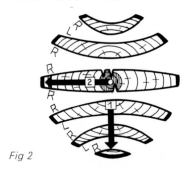

Fig 2

6

Designations: The left side (L) of the board is called the sapwood, and the right (R) the heart side.

The drawings are exaggerated for greater clarity.

A board can of course also warp lengthwise. It can twist and turn (become warped). As the shape changes during seasoning, so do the dimensions. Width and thickness of the boards decrease. Changes in length are without significance for your purposes.

Which kinds of wood are best for carving?

The wide range of home-grown and foreign woods available gives us plenty to choose from. To begin with, however, a few essential types will be enough. Discussing the properties of wood is not a great deal of use, and practical trials are more instructive. You must get the feel of the wood and see how it responds, whether it cuts well or badly. It will either encourage you to carry on carving or prove unsuitable.

Hardwood is unsuitable for hand carving — your wrist and knife will soon give up the unequal struggle. Softwood can be exciting — but not always, because many types of soft-wood split no matter how sharp the knife is, especially when you carve against the grain. Brittle, grainy wood will quickly discourage you. The lime tree produces excellent wood — soft, yet even, and firm to cut. It does not fray or split. The wood of young trees is whitish, that of old trees reddish. The grain stands out

well without being obtrusive. Whole generations of wood carvers have created magnificent works of art from this material.

Oak is used for outdoor work which will be exposed to the elements. This austere and strong material is one of the hardwoods and resists the weather. A mallet is generally used for working it, but a skilled wood carver will have no difficulty in hand carving small subjects even with this wood. The colour of oak is yellow-brown to yellow-red, and the pores of the wood give it a surface of characteristically attractive appearance.

In mountainous regions pine is a very popular material for carving. It is very resinous, and many years of growth in an exposed position make it especially dense — i.e. fine-ringed — and it is therefore suitable for carving the most delicate figures.

Maple, which is light and hard, and at first glance can almost be mistaken for lime, is recommended for the carving of reliefs, lettering, bowls and particularly trinkets.

Hardwood can be used for belt buckles, ornamental buttons and similar objects subjected to hard wear. Here you will find both beech and walnut useful.

These types of wood will be enough to begin with. They offer an introduction to the medium and are the starting point from which other, less familiar kinds of wood can be tackled. Once you have acquired sufficient skill you will be able to cope with all varieties. The sympathetic nature of the material and the wide range of tools and possible working techniques make wood-carving an easy and attractive craft.

Sawing and seasoning the wood

Boards or planks are bought in the timber yard and cut up into handy lengths at home. Wood of $1\frac{3}{8}$, $1\frac{5}{8}$, $2-2\frac{3}{8}$ and $2\frac{3}{4}-3\frac{1}{4}$ in. or 3·5, 4, 5–6 and 7–8 cm. thickness is quite sufficient. If no gluing is intended the wood can be taken from a freshly-felled tree trunk and used for small figures immediately. But if the wood is to be joined and glued, it must be very thoroughly seasoned. As a rough guide, $\frac{3}{8}$ in. or 1 cm. thickness of wood requires one year's seasoning.

It is almost impossible to store entire logs as raw material without their splitting in the course of the seasoning process. You can keep the splits within tolerable limits if you leave the bark on the log and cover the end-grained face. Storage on trestles, i.e. away from the ground, is recommended, and the log should be turned repeatedly. Drilling the pith out of short sections (Fig. 3) and leaving this portion uncovered is a protection well worth taking.

A sculpture in the round does not require that the wood should be seasoned. Ideally you should begin carving immediately after the tree has been felled. Roughing out from all sides and hollowing the work wherever possible will eliminate the internal stress from the green wood and reduce later seasoning cracks to a tolerable minimum.

For large sculptures (from a single block), trunks stored in their original condition are very suitable. Two stout planks are obtained when the trunk is sawn straight through (Fig. 4). Quarter sawing also produces good strong material (Fig. 5), which seasons with very few cracks.

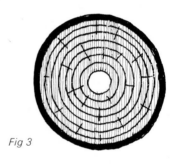

Fig 3

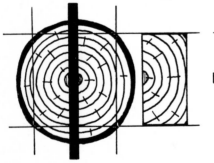

Fig 4

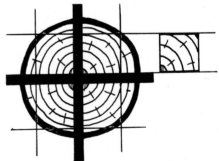

Fig 5

The tools

A carving knife and three chisels are the only tools you need to begin with. These tools will enable you to carve the first practice subjects in the book without difficulty.

Additional tools make the carving easier; they make the more detailed rendering of a figure possible. The tools Q and R, p. 10 are very useful if you want to carve larger figures; why should you work harder than necessary with tools that are too small for the purpose?

The carving knife has a wide variety of uses, and is particularly suitable for chip-carved ornaments. The tools called fluters easily enter the wood when given a rotary movement, and are particularly suitable for hollowing. The shallow gouges are used for deeper penetration in roughing-out work, as are the chisels, which also have a special use in the field of chip carving (and letter carving). The parting tool is a chip-carving tool, but it is also useful for detailed work on figures. The bent gouge is used for deep hollowing where chips can no longer be effectively removed with a straight gouge.

These hints only offer a rough outline of the uses of the various tools for the applications of the tools can overlap a great deal.

Note: the capital letters identifying the carving tools refer to this book only; they are not standard designations.

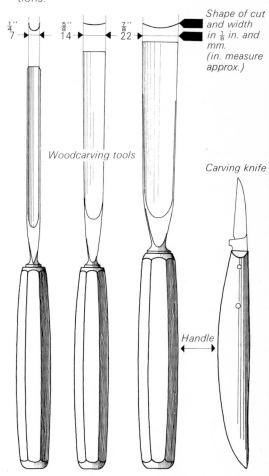

Shape of cut and width in $\frac{1}{8}$ in. and mm. (in. measure approx.)

Woodcarving tools

Carving knife

Handle

9

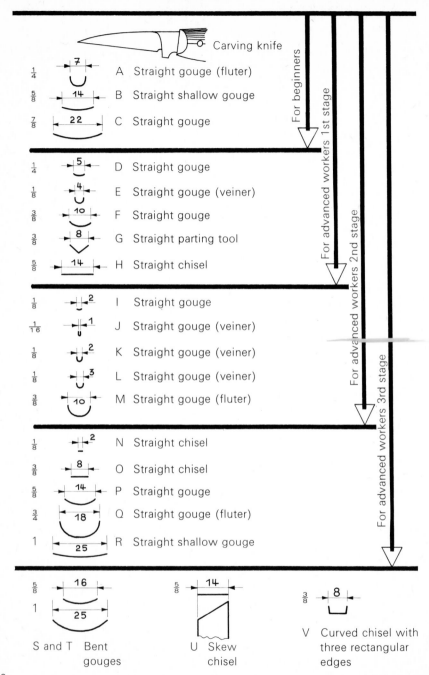

Carving knife

$\frac{1}{4}$ — A Straight gouge (fluter) — 7

$\frac{5}{8}$ — B Straight shallow gouge — 14

$\frac{7}{8}$ — C Straight gouge — 22

For beginners 1st stage

$\frac{1}{4}$ — D Straight gouge — 5

$\frac{1}{8}$ — E Straight gouge (veiner) — 4

$\frac{3}{8}$ — F Straight gouge — 10

$\frac{3}{8}$ — G Straight parting tool — 8

$\frac{5}{8}$ — H Straight chisel — 14

For advanced workers 1st stage

$\frac{1}{8}$ — I Straight gouge — 2

$\frac{1}{16}$ — J Straight gouge (veiner) — 1

$\frac{1}{8}$ — K Straight gouge (veiner) — 2

$\frac{1}{8}$ — L Straight gouge (veiner) — 3

$\frac{3}{8}$ — M Straight gouge (fluter) — 10

For advanced workers 2nd stage

$\frac{1}{8}$ — N Straight chisel — 2

$\frac{3}{8}$ — O Straight chisel — 8

$\frac{5}{8}$ — P Straight gouge — 14

$\frac{3}{4}$ — Q Straight gouge (fluter) — 18

1 — R Straight shallow gouge — 25

For advanced workers 3rd stage

$\frac{5}{8}$ 1 — 16, 25 — S and T Bent gouges

$\frac{5}{8}$ — 14 — U Skew chisel

$\frac{3}{8}$ — 8 — V Curved chisel with three rectangular edges

10

Sharpening the tools

A badly-tuned musical instrument spoils all the fun of playing; a blunt carving tool is equally discouraging and is usually the main cause if one's initial enthusiasm for carving rapidly wanes. Blunt tools scrape the wood, tear off splinters and make an unpleasant sound when cutting. Before you begin carving the tools must be razor sharp, otherwise there is little point in starting.

Long-bevelled tools are used because they enter the wood quickly and smoothly. If you work with a mallet, however, the bevel should be shorter, though obviously never as short as that of the chisels used for stone and metal working.

The main sharpening process is carried out with a manual or power-driven grinder; but this is not enough and must always be followed by wet honing on an Arkansas or oilstone. Often a fine burr will remain on the edge after sharpening, and this can be carefully pushed off with the tip of one's finger. Inside sharpening of gouges is done with a slipstone. Final stropping with a leather strop can work wonders.

You would be well advised to learn to sharpen your own tools, since taking them to be sharpened every time they become a little blunt will prove a tedious process. The purchase of the necessary implements is well worth while, especially since a small manual tool grinder, an oilstone and a few slipstones are really quite cheap. If you are the owner of an electric grinder you will of course use this for coarse grinding; it is quicker and leaves both hands free to hold the tool. Small belt grinders are also particularly suitable.

Start with a coarse grain, and change over to a fine grain. To prevent overheating immerse the tool regularly in a container full of water; the edge on a thin carving tool is quickly burned. The utmost care must be taken during honing — this cannot be emphasised often enough. Note: all tools bought new must be specially honed before they are used for the first time. The following illustrations give further information.

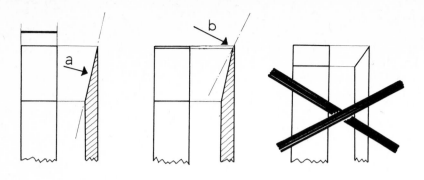

(a) Grind a long bevel with the grinder.
(b) Sharpen finely with the oilstone. The third example shows a carving tool with too short a bevel.

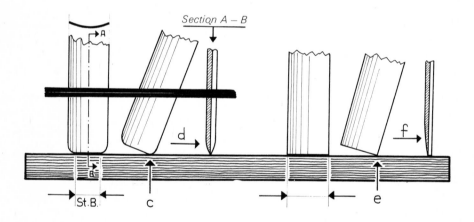

(c) Incorrectly sharpened tool with rounded edges. The reduced cutting width is a disadvantage in carving.

(d) Too short and convex bevel is an additional fault.

(e) Straight-honed tool with full cutting width on the wood. When edged, it immediately attacks the wood accurately and keenly and produces a clean incision.

(f) The long bevel ensures excellent entry into the wood.

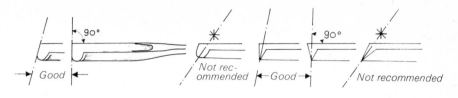

Good | Not recommended | Good | Not recommended

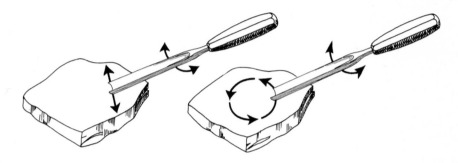

Honing on the oilstone. The arrows indicate the rotary movement of the tools and the direction of simultaneous movement on the stone.

The edge does not touch the stone

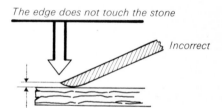

Incorrect

Steep position of the long-bevelled tool ensures good sharpening. If the position is too flat and the bevel too short, the desired sharpness cannot be obtained.

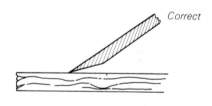

Correct

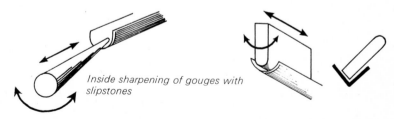

Inside sharpening of gouges with slipstones

13

How to hold the tools when hand-carving

Pure hand carving is done without a mallet, and a carpenter's bench, too, is unnecessary. All you need are your hands and a sharp knife or carving tool. The left hand holds the wood in position, the right hand guides the tool. It does not grip the handle, but the shaft of the tool as in the first illustration. This may look clumsy, but appearances are deceptive — even the most delicate sculptural details can be carved in this manner. The fingers never become fatigued and the strength of the whole hand can be brought to bear. The edge of the carving hand constantly presses against the work, preventing it from suddenly slipping. Grip the tool as close to the edge as possible and never advance it so far that it will touch and injure the other hand, which should hold the work in such a way that it is always protected from the carving tool. Hands, tool and work now form a precisely co-ordinated unit. Avoid cramped postures from the very beginning; work in the most relaxed and restful manner possible. Your hand-hold will continuously change as the bottom illustration shows. Here the fourth and little fingers, always at the ready, act as a brake and prevent the tool from slipping.

The third picture shows how not to do it. If the tool slips the left hand will be badly injured. Grasp the handle only when using a mallet.

Carving with the knife consists of four main techniques (see illustrations

I Correct

II Correct

14

A to D): A — away from the body; B — towards the body; C — with thumb pressure; D — with the point of the blade. Thoroughly practise C in particular until you are familiar with this technique.

III Incorrect

(A) Carving away from the body. This free method of cutting has been found very useful for rapid and bold roughing out. Long, thick chips can be removed in this manner. Avoid sweeping movements.

(B) Carving towards the body. The thumb supports the wood; this makes more delicate and detailed carving possible.

15

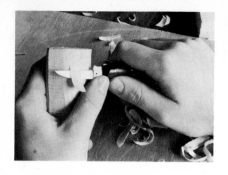

(C) Carving with thumb pressure. Here the thumb assists in the carving by pressure on the blade. This method alternated with (B) produces good, efficient work.

(D) Carving with the point of the blade. The steeply angled position is designed for carving the details of figures. Surface carvings can also be done in this way.

Carving with a mallet

This method differs from pure hand carving in that you need both hands for holding the tools. The work is held in a clamping device, preferably a carpenter's vice. The figure is clamped between the jaws and carved in a horizontal position. The upright position is by no means wrong, but here you must allow for the 'bounce' at every blow of the mallet. The clamping jaws have the additional disadvantage that they leave bruises. Before the figure is finished, small slips of wood should therefore be inserted between it and the jaws.

Alternatively, a bench screw can be used, and for this any heavy table will be suitable. The simplest method is to screw a robust piece of wood to the underside of the work, and to secure this in turn to the table with two clamps.

Unless the bench screw is screwed very deep into the work, it will become loose after the first few blows. Accordingly, a deep and narrow hole must be drilled, in such a way that the screw does not interfere with the carving.

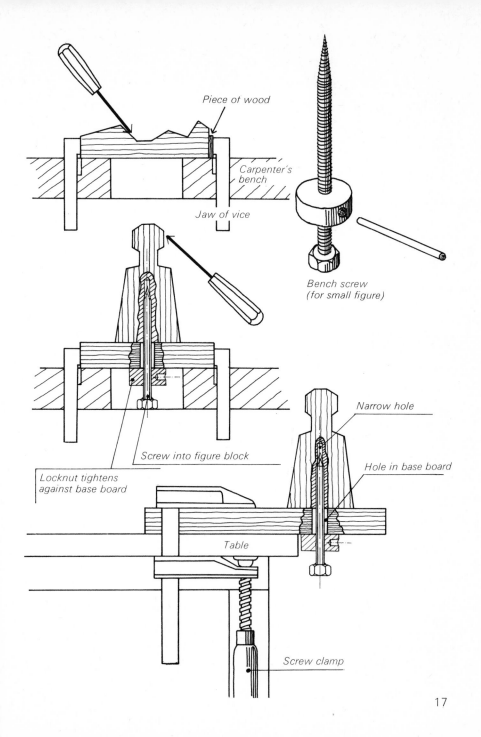

Piece of wood

Carpenter's bench

Jaw of vice

Bench screw (for small figure)

Screw into figure block

Locknut tightens against base board

Narrow hole

Hole in base board

Table

Screw clamp

First carving exercises

You should not begin by trying to realise ideas or by copying existing models for practice. Most beginners set their aims far too high, and the result is generally failure. When you build a house you start with the foundations if it is not to collapse later.

According to an old sculptor's saying, the finished figure is already in the unworked block; all the sculptor has to do is free them from the surrounding material. To reach this goal, you first

have to practise 'carving away'.

Take a small block and carve away at it until only chips are left. Repeat this with several blocks until you have become proficient in handling the tool. It is important to try out the different carving tools in order to become familiar with their specific cutting properties. The smaller the block becomes the more carefully must you handle the tool. This is how you learn to carve. Do not chip away frantically; a form will emerge spontaneously if you use the carving tool in a relaxed and playful manner.

If you enter into the idea of this accidental form and carve it into a finished piece, you will have completed your first abstract subject. Many an acknowledged work of art has been accidentally created in this way.

To begin with, experiments with shapes are enough. You will not yet be capable of rendering an imaged form in your raw material. Copying a model, too, will usually be a pathetic failure, because of the fear of cutting away too much. Naturally, practice and experience in handling the carving tool are not acquired in a day.

Good carving exercises: shaping and hollowing lengths of wood

First cut out some attractive irregular shapes with a saw. Hollow them roughly, rather than closely following the outlines, first marking out the hollows with a pencil. Start gouging with a straight gouge; go as deep as you can with this tool. There is no need at this stage to strive for a particularly clean cut. You can produce original bowls and vessels in this way.

The bent gouge is used for the fining-down operation of hollowing. It is the only tool capable of normal chip-removing in deeply recessed areas. Without it only shallow hollows can be carved. Any rough areas which remain inaccessible to this tool can be scraped with the gouge. Sandpapering is also quite acceptable, affording a different

treatment of the material. However, once an object has been sandpapered, it is no longer suitable for carving, and will rapidly blunt the tools.

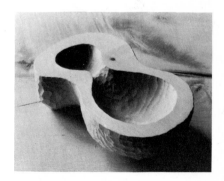

Underside.

Surface treatment

Hand finishing the wood with the carving tool produces a surface consisting of many individual tool cuts. Depending on the fineness of the cuts as well as on the types of tool used, this surface finish considerably influences the character of a wood carving.

This carved sphere illustrates the technical terms used.

Avoid a monotonous finish. A variety of carved facets of different sizes will enliven the finished piece.

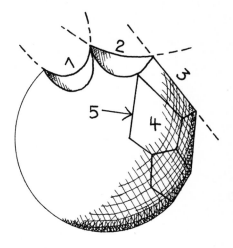

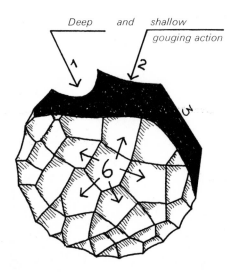

Deep   and   shallow
gouging action

(1) Deep gouging cut.
(2) Shallow gouging cut.
(3) Plain cut.
(4) Facet (produced by a single cut).
(5) Cut edge (boundary of carved area).
(6) All facets and cut edges together produce the surface finish.

The main carved edge and the main carved plane as creative elements

The area of the main carved plane includes a number of facets in the surface finish. The main carved edge outlines this enlarged plane and raises it to the level of a formal element of the carving. The carved edge has a creative function. Even after the figure has been smoothed it remains visible on the surface as a prominent, important feature of emphasis. During roughing out the main carved edge plays a decisive part, helping to establish the form clearly, in bold outlines.

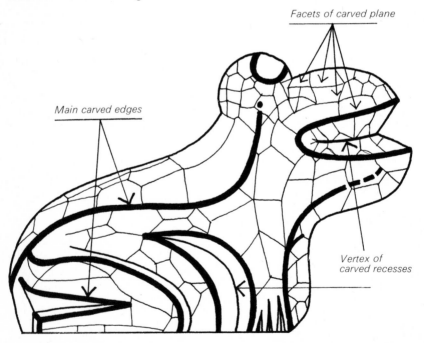

Facets of carved plane

Main carved edges

Vertex of carved recesses

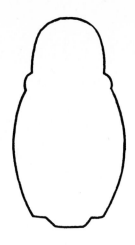

Dimensions 3 × 1¾ × 2 in. or 7·4 × 4·2 × 4·9 cm.

In the sketch of a figure it is the most important line, indicating the roughing-out cut that transforms the original block into a shape.

Files, rasps, sandpaper

Carving in relation to the grain

A rugged surface finish is not suitable for all carvings. In most female figures, for instance, a harsh network of carved facets would only be disturbing. This is why you must either use the finest carving tools for finishing or smooth the figure down until the only surface feature is the grain of the wood. If the figure has softly flowing lines the specifically feminine character will be further emphasised. Austere modern sculptures, reduced to bold shapes, often also lend themselves to smooth surface treatment. The frequently heard objection that this destroys the sculptor's personal note is unfounded. The character of a sculpture is primarily determined by the idea behind it; the correct choice of surface finish, although important, is only a supporting feature. Whether you choose a smooth surface or one with carved facets depends above all on your subject.

If you have decided that the carving should be smoothed, first remove the facets (not the intersections of the main planes) with a file and a rasp. Follow this up with coarse and then fine sandpaper.

Wood cannot be worked equally well from all directions. This is an experience every beginner has during his very first practice. Sometimes the tool enters the wood readily with a clean, chip-removing cut, then again it meets resistance. This phenomenon is due to the direction of the cut in relation to the grain. In the first case, the directions of cut and grain coincide; in the second they do not, and we can speak of 'incorrect' carving.

The direction of the grain is evident from the texture of the wood. In the course of time the practised woodcarver will become so used to it that it will be second nature to him to apply his carving tool always in the right direction. If you have not yet reached this stage, just carry on carving without worrying about such problems — but keep your eyes open. The resistance the wood offers will soon indicate the direction in which you have to carve. Small carved figures are eminently suitable for this purpose, since you need only turn the work to find the right direction again. The following illustrations demonstrate the importance of this question.

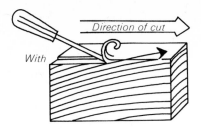

Carving with the grain.

The cutting direction is identical with that of the grain, or runs slightly across it. The latter is the ideal cutting direction. Because the grain runs outwards, the chips come away easily and the carved surface is smooth and shiny.

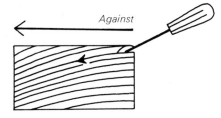

Carving against the grain.

The tool is hampered by the grain running into the wood and the chips come away only with difficulty if at all. The carved surface is rough and matt.

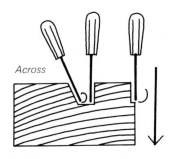

Carving across the grain.

When you cut very steeply or vertically across the grain the chip will always come away well, but a scooping movement of the gouge will be necessary. The wood feels harder and additional force is needed.

Practising what you have learned

If you want to finish plane (A) in a longitudinal direction, you will have to change the cutting direction once to achieve a uniformly good result. This is because after the boundary line the grain turns back into the wood. If you maintained your original cutting direction, you would get a poor finish.

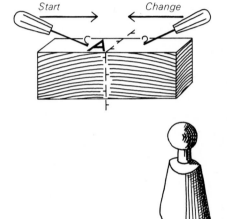

Examples of cutting directions on figures

It is most instructive to draw sketches of simple examples like this one and try to find the right cutting direction on them. An arrow represents the movements of the carving knife.

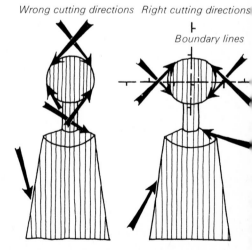

Wrong cutting directions *Right cutting directions*

Boundary lines

Sawn blocks and technical drawings

Sketches of ideas translated into technical drawings are sometimes indispensable in carving. You are urgently advised to study this chapter in detail, because exact outlines are a great help when you cut out the wood with a saw and later, when you carve the plastic figures.

The following questions arise when you make a sketch: how do you establish exact outlines of ideas, designs, or models from which to make blocks, for the cutting-out of a wood?

Carvers often go no further than cutting out the most important outlines with a saw. Naturally there are some designs that permit the preparation of the figure from further aspects. Once a model has been designed it is simple to transfer the desired outlines

by tracing its contours on a sheet of cardboard or paper. But if the sketch model is three-dimensional the necessary two-dimensional aspects must first be developed from it.

As in technical drawing, enough aspects and sections are drawn so that the object holds no more secrets and can be carved with the aid of these varied representations.

The most important aspects are the front elevation, the plan, and the side elevation. Since we are dealing not with machines, technical implements, and buildings, but figures such as humans, animals, symbols etc., let us use different terms for these aspects: let us call the front elevation main aspect, the ground plan top view, and the side elevation profile.

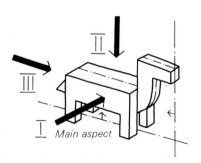

Main aspect

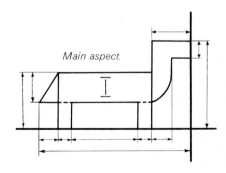

Main aspect.

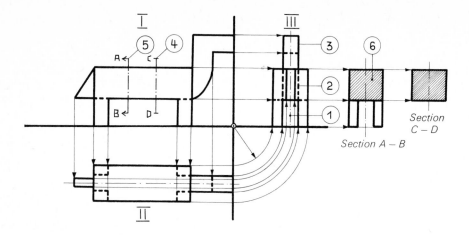

Section C – D

Section A – B

This is only natural, since it would be odd to speak of the ground plan of an animal. That the conventional main aspect of a creature can become the profile owing to the technical approach of the draughtsman need not disturb you.

The main aspect is always the side that yields the most clues for the development of the other aspects. For instance: the rough quadruped designed from a sketch model shows most of its body from the side.

The projection axes are derived from descriptive geometry and drawn as the first features on a piece of paper. The principal axes (or centre lines) of the animal are now lined up parallel to the projection axes, and the main aspect drawn in accordingly.

Beginning from the main aspect draw fine auxiliary lines from all edges and corners downwards as well as laterally and thus develop other aspects. The side view is completed with the aid of the circular arc section.

(1) Centre line (auxiliary line for lining up).

(2) Invisible edges and corners.
(3) Visible edges and corners.
(4) Site of cut without arrows (draw only the cut plane).
(5) Site of cut with arrows in the viewing line (everything visible from this direction is included in the drawing).
(6) Cut plane (this is hatched; invisible edges and corners are only exceptionally entered in this plane).

The side view (III) now presents the animal's hindquarters (the tail). If you want to look at the animal's front, you must line up the main view with the projection axes so that the head points towards the left (or simply projects the side view to the left instead of to the right). This is mentioned only to further a more detailed appreciation of 'technical seeing'. For the blocks to be cut out with the saw you need only the outlines, identical in both side views.

The required blocks are cut out very much in the manner of black paper silhouettes according to the aspects obtained.

Later the auxiliary lines are omitted

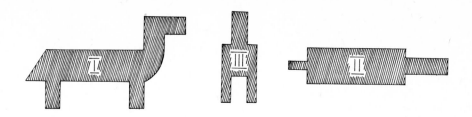

from the drawing and the points necessary for the construction transferred with dividers. To get an idea (or insight) of the cross section of a certain part of the body, section it before your mind's eye through the relevant plane. On the animal the drawing was made on the trunk, and thus the section obtained.

The example of a matchbox will clearly demonstrate to you what you have learned. Place the box on a piece of paper, broadside parallel to you. The imprint is the main aspect. Trace the contours with a pencil. Tilt it downwards through 90° to obtain the top view, return it to its previous position and tilt it to the right for the side view.

This is how you obtain the cut-out blocks from the clay models.

You can also make technical drawings of planned figures with round features without difficulty. The advantage here is that the outlines directly indicate the blocks to be sawn out. Examples of these are the working drawings of the models of studies in this book. The lines of these drawings consist of the contours discussed in this chapter, in addition to the lines of the main cut edges and the corners of the cut planes of the planned figures. If an edge or corner line ends in a rounded surface, mark this transition with dots or dashes as the end of a sharp edge or a sharp corner.

Making a rough figure

Begin with a piece of wood of the right size, which we shall call a figure block. For large projects you may need to glue together several pieces. Prepare paper or cardboard patterns of the main aspects of the figure: front, side and possibly top view. Then trace these onto the block with a soft pencil. The front view is sawn out first, and where the other outlines are obliterated by this operation, they should be restored by drawing round the pattern again.

When several figures are to be carved (e.g. a Nativity scene), patterns are a very welcome aid to dividing up the available wood, and waste is reduced to a minimum.

The framed numbers on the illustrations below indicate the sequence of the sawing-out operations: 1 — front view; 2 — side view. With some figures

a third sawing operation can be added. Do not forget the prop (arrow), to ensure that the wood is firmly supported on the machine bench.

Sawing is best done with a band- or jigsaw; the jigsaw is particularly handy for piercing carvings. If these useful tools are not available, you can if the figures are small make do with a hand-saw. Roughing out a figure from a block with the carving tools is much too laborious; take it to a joiner or carpenter if you do not have the right equipment. The reasonably priced power tool kits available from do-it-yourself shops are well worth considering in this context.

With a power saw one can easily cut round shapes and remove large masses of material. But any rashness or negligence may result in the fast-working

machine whipping the work from your hands and causing you injuries. Always avoid endangering your fingers, but grasp the work firmly where it is safe to do so. If you hold it lightly or indecisively you will risk trouble instead of avoiding it — always ensure, therefore, that the work is firmly supported.

First cut out the side view of the animal, follow this with a bold outline of the top view, and lastly cut the main details of the body. Beginners should at first omit the third stage, and include the cutting-out of the recesses (see arrows) in the second stage.

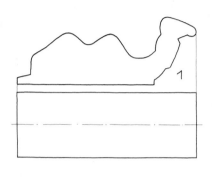

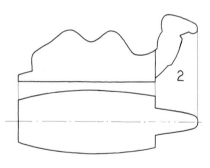

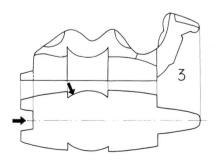

The correct direction of grain in a block

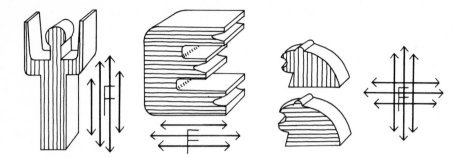

In the interests of maximum structural rigidity the figures must not be cut from the wood at random; make sure that the grain runs in the right direction. An example: if you carve an animal with slender legs the grain must run parallel to them, otherwise they will break while they are being carved.

In the thick and strong portions of a figure the direction of the grain plays a minor role. Attention must be paid to thin and protruding parts. In the illustrations, for example, the structural rigidity of the animal's legs is more important than that of the open mouth (arrow M).

Unless other reasons militate against it, the direction of the grain in solid figures without projecting parts is unimportant. The sheaf of arrows symbol F will appear throughout the rest of the book and indicate in each case the direction of the grain or fibres in the figure to be carved as illustrated here.

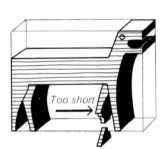

Wrong direction of grain in block. The legs are very liable to break as the grain running across them is too short

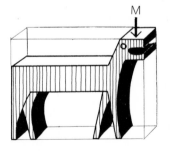

Right direction of grain in block. The grain extends along the legs

Preparing the wood for gluing

A figure carved out of a single piece of wood represents the ideal case. This is partly because the grain and the tint of the wood will then be even. Figures consisting of several pieces of wood glued together tend to have flaws and to suffer from faulty craftsmanship. There is a risk of appreciable differences in the colour of the wood, and of well defined and subdued grain texture meeting along the joints.

Unfortunately the joining and gluing together of pieces of wood cannot be altogether avoided, especially with all large projects. Even if a stout tree yields a relief panel of suitable width, bad warping or tearing will greatly reduce its usefulness in the natural state.

It is therefore essential to study and master the purely technical preparations of joining.

Boards and planks must not be joined haphazardly. Warping of the wood must be allowed for, the grain and natural colour of the pieces to be joined must match. If possible wood from the same trunk should therefore be used.

Only well seasoned wood is suitable for joining and gluing.

During trimming close attention must be paid to cupping and seasoning cracks. Unavoidable knots are allotted spaces where they are ultimately invisible – or where they are not disturbing. Never forget to allow for size. The wood from the timber yard, cut into rough shape, is left to stand in the workshop for a few more days to give it another chance to relieve any remaining stresses.

After these precautions the wood can be safely machine-planed.

The wood is now sorted and the matched pieces marked with symbols or numbers for identification. (See next page: joining a relief panel.)

(1) The side boards are correctly joined. All right sides face each other and the sapwood sides are adjacent.

(2) If boards are made narrower, the working face of the relief panel will be less inclined to bulge.

(3) The right sides of the boards are best suited for relief panels. They never warp. Their even grain is an added advantage. It will not be very conspicuous in the relief.

(4) This is wrong. The heart is glued to the sapwood. There will be a serious risk of the glued joint opening up because of the wood warping in different directions.

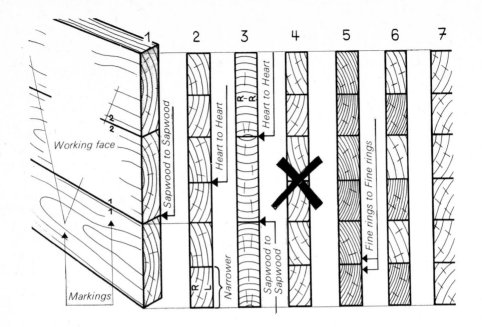

Working face

Markings

1   2   3   4   5   6   7

Sapwood to Sapwood

Heart to Heart

Heart to Heart

R-R

Narrower

R L

Sapwood to Sapwood

Fine rings to Fine rings

(5) Only uniform wood has been joined together.

(6) For special projects a rhythmical change in the surface texture may be desirable.

(7) The plate is compensated by the alternate concave and convex warping of the boards. (Note the rays in the illustration.)

In a figure block the glued surfaces are large. Obviously, here much stronger forces are at work than in the joining of a relief panel. The forces involved in the warping of the wood are immense. Their direction can be clearly seen in its warping body, and advantage should be taken of them in the joining process.

On its left side the wood becomes hollow, on the right side it bulges out. If you join the right sides of two boards or planks together there is a great likelihood that the glued joint will open up again. The forces of the wood acting in opposite directions pull the joint apart (see Fig. 1).

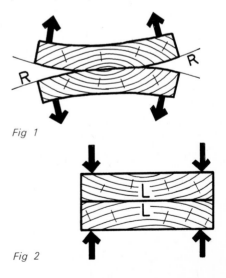

R   R

Fig 1

L
L

Fig 2

34

A trick is therefore used: the left sides are glued together. The force of the wood now compresses the glued joint (see Fig. 2). Alternatively the left and right sides of the boards can be glued together so that they warp (or 'ride') in the same direction (see Fig. 3).

Experience has shown that with good workmanship the advantage outweighs the small risk.

When joining a third board one can join all the boards in such a way that they warp (or 'ride') in the same direction (see Fig. 4). This method produces uniform structure, which is an advantage with figures in natural colours.

Alternatively when three boards are joined, two of them may face each other with their right sides as in Fig. 5 (correspondingly the fourth to be glued will have a left-to-left joint, again see Fig. 5). The reason for this exception is that the force of the wood is already absorbed (weakened) by the one or two left-to-left joints. The two inside boards can be further restrained if they are sawn up.

Heartwood with its vertical annual rings occupies a special position and can be joined and glued without fear of any mishap (see Fig. 6).

Here is another basic fact: making a relief panel or a figure block always involves a certain risk. Even the experienced worker will be continuously faced with new tasks. Be that as it may, these examples of joining and gluing are basic directions for taming the wood. That slipshod and indifferent work will invite failure from the outset goes without saying.

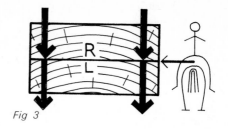

Fig 3

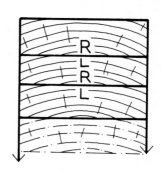

Fig 4

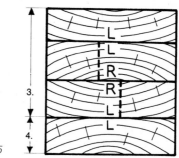

Fig 5

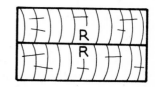

Fig 6

35

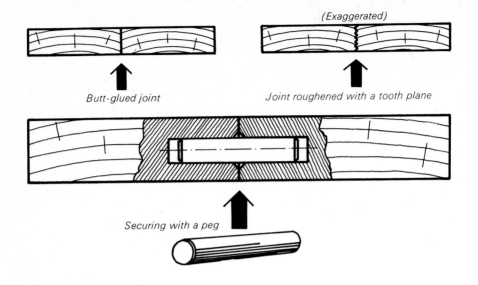

(Exaggerated)

Butt-glued joint   *Joint roughened with a tooth plane*

Securing with a peg

Securing the joints

The wood the sculptor joins and glues is mostly very strong. It therefore is, despite complete seasoning, still temperamental. Its drawback continues to be the swelling and shrinking depending on the degree of atmospheric humidity; this is a constant source of trouble.

A butt-joint is not secure. This can be changed with a tooth plane; the roughened glue-covered faces will then engage like teeth, thereby strengthening the connection.

For most glued joints, the peg is used for strengthening. It has been found very reliable. All you need for it is a handbrace and a few screw augers. Pegs can be easily made, particularly with a peg runner. They can also be bought in the form of rods, and consist of well seasoned beech or ash. The peg holes must of course always be drilled so that they do not conflict with the subsequent shaping operations.

The making of peg holes

This is a minor problem that needs your brief attention. Even small deviations in the matching hole will cause trouble in practice — trouble which can be avoided. Example: first mark the sites of the intended holes on piece A and drive a little nail into each; snip off the heads of the nails. By pressing the two pieces of wood together you will obtain the markings of the corresponding holes in piece B.

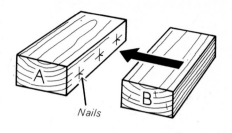

Nails

Some advice on gluing

The pieces of wood are pressed together with screw clamps. During the cold season, the surfaces to be glued together are slightly warmed before adhesive is applied. Any radiator is suitable for this purpose.

The commercially available cold glue raises the fewest problems, but with light woods it has the slight disadvantage of somewhat discolouring the edges of the joint.

Warm glue has an advantage in this respect — although it is a little more complicated and difficult to use. After boiling, this adhesive must be really thin-bodied, applied and then the pieces glued together very quickly.

The clamps are tightened with all force. The glue must be pressed into the pores of the wood and not be left as a thin film in the joint. It is better to use too many than too few screw clamps. The glue forced out of the joint must be wiped off at once with a wet sponge; ensure that the joint makes firm contact everywhere. When the clamps are tightened firmly enough, the pieces must be so close together that a glued joint is almost invisible.

Allow the joint at least six to eight hours to set before you continue carving.

Carving a figure

The models which follow are drawn so that the important details are clearly visible. They are represented technically rather than three-dimensionally, so that they can also be used as plans for the production of the block. The various aspects show the outlines of the final figure, and can be traced to obtain working patterns for cutting out with the power saw. The dimensions given are for small practice models; they are intended for guidance only, and there is no need to stick to them exactly.

Your main guide to the final shape of the figures will be the accompanying photographs. They supplement the drawings, and the two together will form an effective basis from which you can work.

The various patterns can be traced from the book pages with tracing paper. The most important pattern in most of the designs which follow is that of the side view. Draw this outline on the wood and cut it out with the saw; this saves much unnecessary manual work with the carving tool. If possible, also cut out the top and end views of the block.

Every drawing includes the sheaf of arrows symbol indicating the correct direction of the grain in the figure.

Crossed arrows indicate that the grain can run in either of two directions. Using the working patterns, the figure block must be traced and cut out of the board so that the direction of the grain is correct.

When producing a figure block, you must approach it visually to see how it can best be executed. Begin by looking at the figure only in terms of the edges and surfaces of its various aspects. Even after it has been sawn out it is useful to sketch in further details with the carving tool on the same principle, and to pass on to rounded modelling only after this possibility has been exhausted. This method follows the visual approach of mechanical draughtsmanship and makes it possible to complete the figure systematically and with confidence. It is such an uncomplicated treatment of the medium that the remaining stage of modelling is little more than a process of rounding off the corners.

The photographs of the mythical beast on the next few pages may serve as an example of a figure taking shape. They show what can be achieved with simple means. The surface finish is a matter of choice — natural faceted finish, scales carved with the gouge, or smooth sandpapered finish.

The design

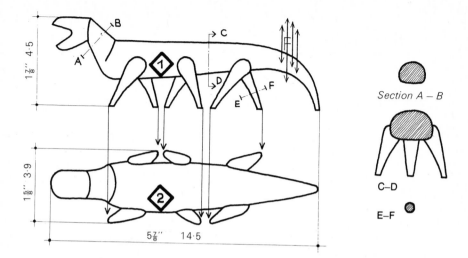

Section A – B

C–D

E–F

All measurements for diagrams in in. and cm.

The figure

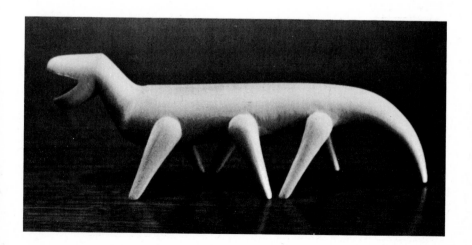

In a figure in the round, all limbs and parts on all sides are properly finished. Although the main emphasis should lie on a single aspect, no view should be neglected.

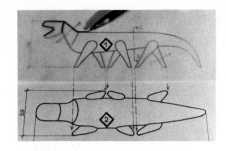

(1a) Trace the design on transparent paper.
(1b) Enlarge it (see page 42).
(1c) Cut out enlarged copies as patterns.

(2a) Place pattern (1) on the lime board, align it correctly with the grain (see sheaf of arrows) and draw round it.
(2b) Cut the figure block off the board.

(3a) Cut out the traced side view (1).
(3b) Trace pattern of top view (2).

(4a) Cut out the top view.
(4b) Mark in the tops of the legs with a pencil.

Now the block is ready for carving. The photographs show how you can save time by working methodically.

(5) Develop the angle of the legs on both sides with the $\frac{5}{8}$ in or 14 mm. shallow gouge (B $\frac{5}{8}$).

(6) Turn the work on its back and cut away the ridges left by the saw (shown hatched) with shallow gouge B $\frac{5}{8}$ and fluter A$\frac{1}{4}$, to free the legs.

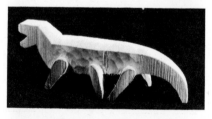

This completes the purely mechanical preparation of the figure. Now we must change to seeing and carving the figure in the round.

(7a) Rough chamfering with bold cuts.

(7b) Finish the entire surface equally boldly (carving knife and shallow gouge B $\frac{5}{8}$).

41

Enlarging a design

Not everybody is skilled enough to undertake the enlargement of a design by sight alone, but it is worth practising. However, if you divide the design into separate parts it will become child's play. To do this, cover the design with a square grid. The intersections between the lines of the sketch and those of the grid at once provide the auxiliary points for the enlargement. The smaller the squares of the grid, the more auxiliary points are obtained. It is a good idea to draw the main vertical and horizontal axes on the design first.

The grid can now be used for the enlargement. Say we wish to obtain a $2\frac{1}{2}$ times enlargement of the small drawing of a nestling. A second grid is drawn with squares $2\frac{1}{2}$ times those of the first. It is now very easy to transfer the auxiliary points from the small to the large grid by sight. The points are then joined to obtain the enlarged nestling, making continued reference to the small drawing to maintain the correct shape. Proportional dividers or a pantograph are also effective and very easy to use.

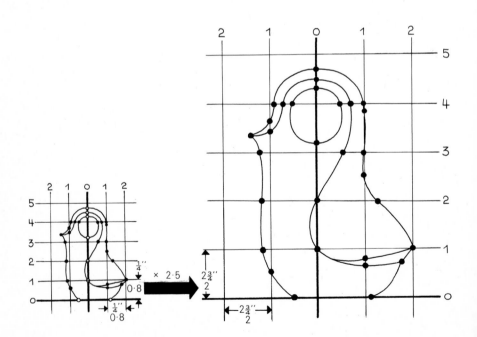

Designs

Nestling

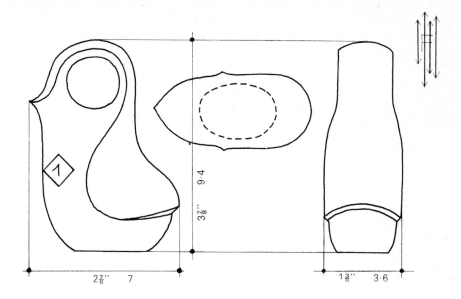

Sitting cat

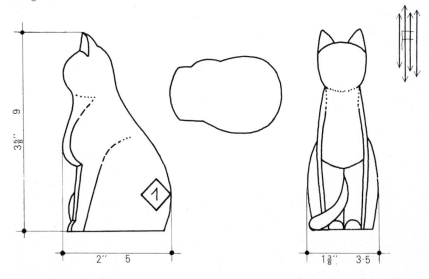

43

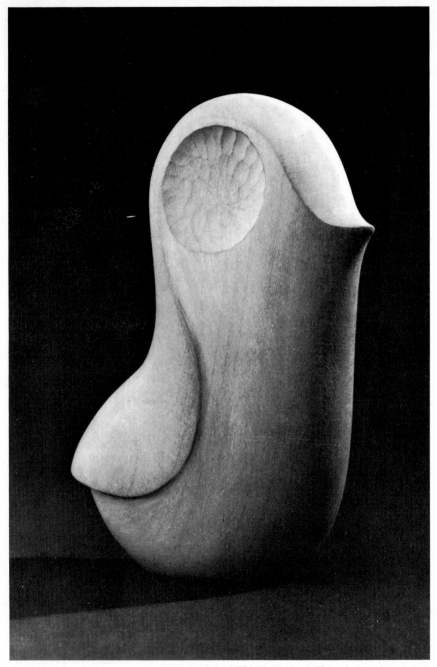

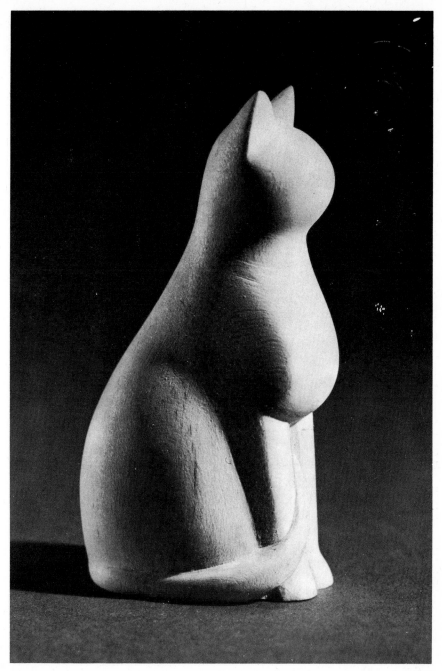

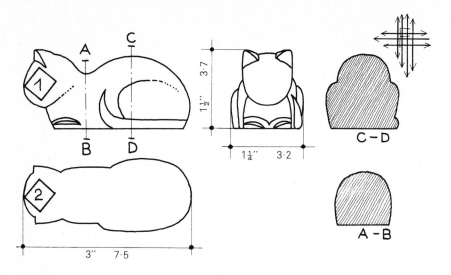

C – D

A – B

The rhinoceros is a typical practice figure for beginners. It consists of a cylindrical trunk supported by four legs.

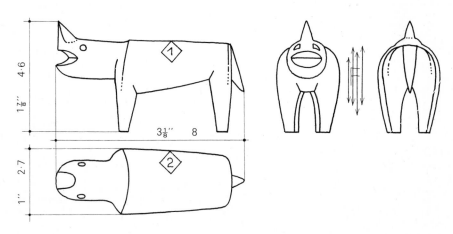

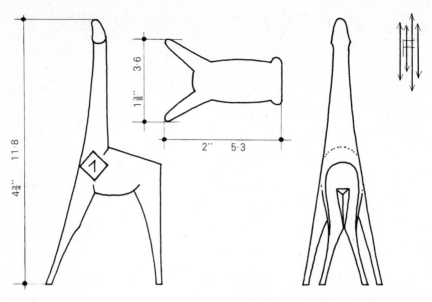

Giraffe

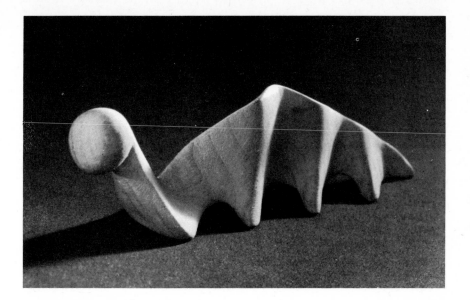

Reptile. The spherical head and the straight neck express the will to move ahead. The body follows in undulating motion. This figure of a serpent gains in impact if it is smoothed as much as possible.

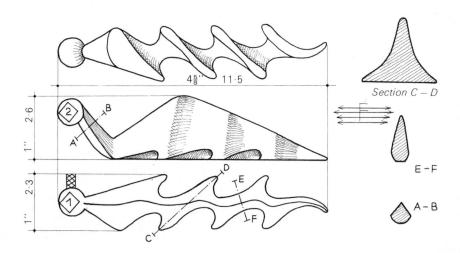

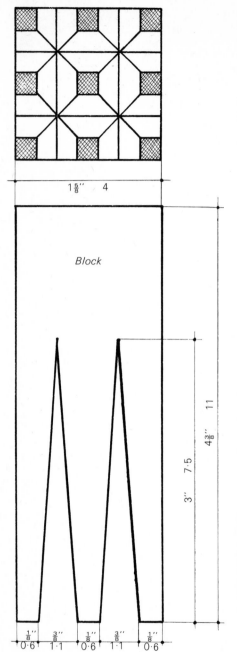

The jellyfish consists of a compact hemisphere supported by nine members. Because of the vertical direction of the grain, the latter could be carved even thinner and finer than they are here. This carving combines simplicity, contrast and appreciation of the raw material into a lively harmony. The knife is used to carve the undulating tentacles.

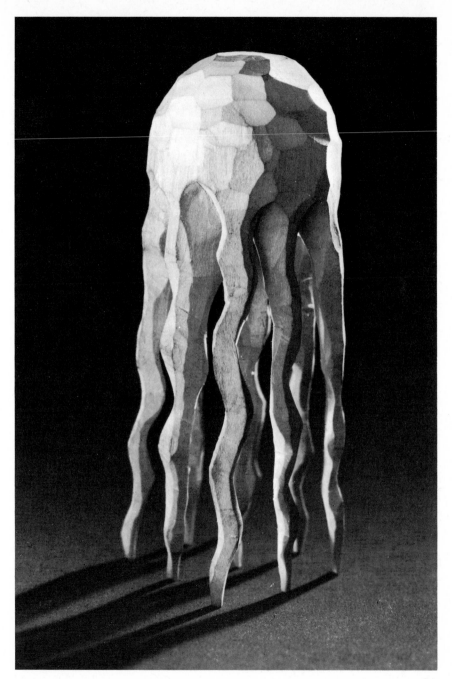

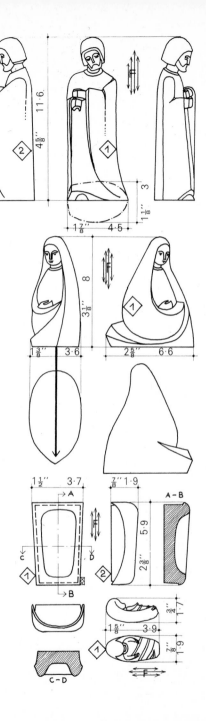

Explanation of the nativity figures.

Mary
A white, undraped shawl envelops the figure, exposing only a hand resting on the body, and the face. The head is slightly inclined towards the manger on the floor and the infant.

Joseph
Here, too, the body is covered by a smooth garb exposing only the head, hands, and one foot.

The staff has been added as an indication of his role as protector. It is pushed through a hole in the fists.

The infant
The little body is swaddled. A fold at the foot end, two ribbons, the free arms, the baby's face only serve to emphasize the form.

The manger
Is a little trough with a cloth spread across. But from the carver's point of view it is only a little block of wood with a carved recess.

Angels
The garments of the thickset figures end in wing stumps. The hands are the only sensitive elements of these figures. They hold a score; the over-long shawms are pushed into the pierced hands. The stylized heads have nothing in common with the 'sweet' angels.

Heavenly vault
The name implies that this is not a stable or a grotto; it is a design based on a symbolical vast space, which surrounds the events in the manger. The Star of Bethlehem is carved in triangular cut into the gently vaulted background of the scene. A few patterns may provide ideas for an extension of the nativity scene. Further examples are the resting sheep and the shepherd.

These carvings are based on the subject 'Music and the Plastic Arts'. As teaching models they should provide ideas for independent studies.

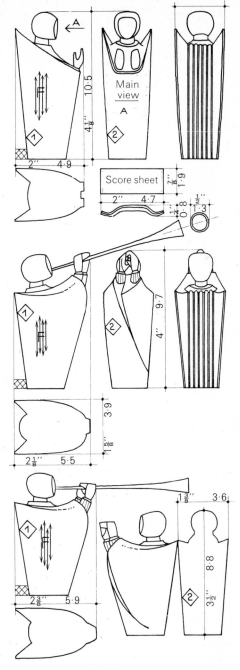

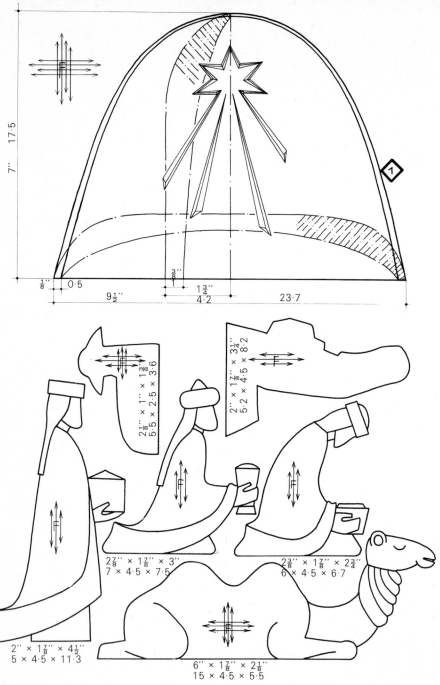

7'' 17·5

$\frac{1}{8}''$ 0·5

$9\frac{1}{2}''$

$\frac{3}{8}''$

$1\frac{3}{4}''$
4·2

23·7

1

$2\frac{1}{8}'' \times 1'' \times 1\frac{3}{8}''$
5·5 × 2·5 × 3·6

$2'' \times 1\frac{7}{8}'' \times 3\frac{1}{4}''$
5·2 × 4·5 × 8·2

$2\frac{7}{8}'' \times 1\frac{7}{8}'' \times 3''$
7 × 4·5 × 7·5

$2\frac{3}{8}'' \times 1\frac{7}{8}'' \times 2\frac{3}{4}''$
6 × 4·5 × 6·7

$2'' \times 1\frac{7}{8}'' \times 4\frac{1}{2}''$
5 × 4·5 × 11·3

$6'' \times 1\frac{7}{8}'' \times 2\frac{1}{8}''$
15 × 4·5 × 5·5

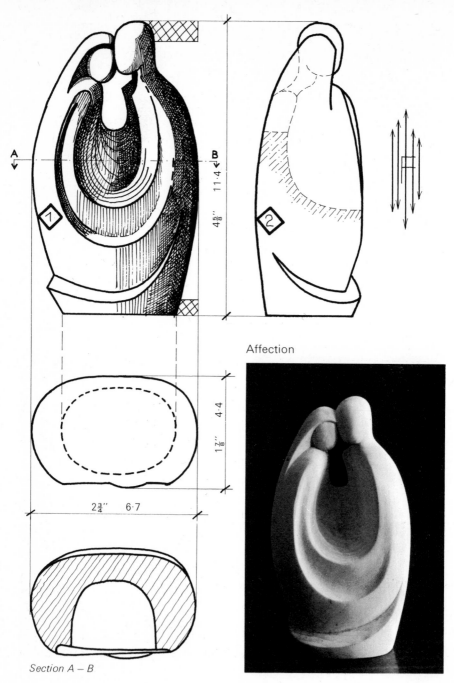

Affection

Section A – B

The singer
Dressed for the festive occasion, she personifies devotion to her art. The score and hands have been developed from the dress. $2\frac{1}{8} \times 1\frac{1}{4} \times 3\frac{3}{8}$ in. or $5 \cdot 5 \times 3 \cdot 2 \times 8 \cdot 6$ cm.

Exuberance
The figures create music and ecstatically accompany the sounds they produce. They are of one piece. $2\frac{1}{8} \times 2 \times 3\frac{3}{8}$ in. or $5 \cdot 7 \times 4 \cdot 8 \times 8 \cdot 4$ cm.

The triplet
A merry trumpet-blowing trio of notes, growing out of a line-patterned garb. $2\frac{3}{4} \times 1\frac{5}{8} \times 4\frac{1}{2}$ in. or $6 \cdot 8 \times 4 \times 11 \cdot 3$ cm.

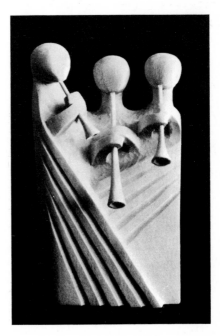

The rising chord
A broadly rising, shallow sound re-
flector supports three notes. A vigorous
plucking of the strings makes them
bring forth a harmonious triad. Correct
direction of the grain permits a fine
carving of the strings. $4\frac{3}{4} \times 1\frac{5}{8} \times 5\frac{5}{8}$ in.
or $11\cdot8 \times 4 \times 14$ cm.

Surface figuring

Since surface texture can have a considerable influence on the appearance of a figure it is advisable to exercise some control over it. This applies particularly when a carving is finely sandpapered.

When a log is sawn through tangentially, the cut surface exhibits a grain with softly flowing lines. A radially- or quarter-sawn log, on the other hand, reveals a grain with sharply defined straight lines. Blocks

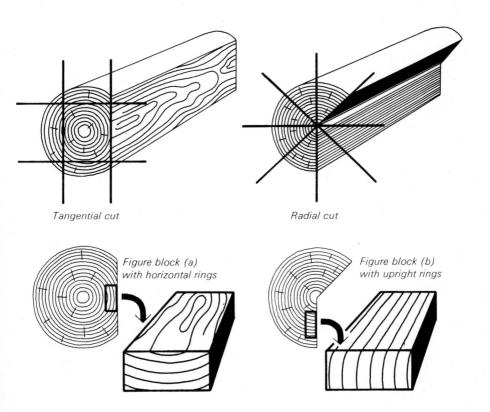

Tangential cut

Radial cut

Figure block (a)
with horizontal rings

Figure block (b)
with upright rings

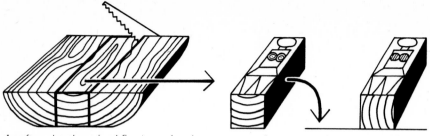

A soft or sharply grained figure can be chosen.

(a) and (b) in the illustration demonstrate the difference. You will see that the two blocks also differ in that the annual rings of block (a) are horizontal on the end-grained face, whereas on block (b) they are vertical. One can thus readily identify the kind of grain of a rough block or board on the end-grained face.

The main aspect of a carving decides its impression on the viewer. The figure blocks are therefore sawn from the board so that these aspects have the characteristics either of the tangential or of the radial cut. With small carvings a figure block with horizontal rings can be tilted on its side, thereby being converted into a block with vertical rings (see above). This gives you the choice of a figure with a soft or sharply defined grain, without the need for cutting a block from another board.

What is the effect of carving into vertical or horizontal rings?

Carve a female figure as an exercise. If the wood shows the tangential cut in the frontal aspect, the surrounding rings are removed and broken by the carving operation. The grain of the breasts will therefore be ring-shaped. If the frontal aspect shows the quarter cut, the rings are not broken by the

carving tool, because they run into the figure. Only deviations and distortions of the lines (D) are possible.

The photograph of the 'R-type' shows the female figure executed strictly in the quarter cut. You will see that the frontal aspect determines the impression given by the figure. The subordinate side views show a soft grain texture here (as of the tangential cut). This type was carved first, to bring out the softness of the 'T-type' all the more strongly in contrast.

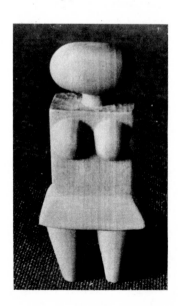

How to make a simple lay figure

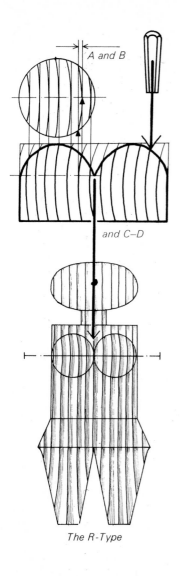

A and B

and C–D

The R-Type

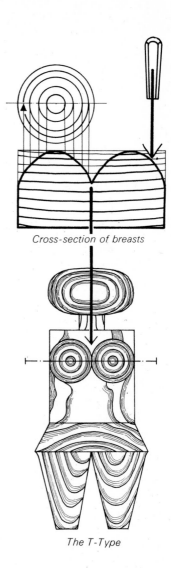

Cross-section of breasts

The T-Type

A simple way of rendering movement

Obviously you need not study the anatomy of the human body. You must, however, consider the skeleton. The skeletons of the medieval woodcuts depicting the 'Dance of Death' are instructive in every respect. They are original both in concept and artistic approach.

Many movements of the human body are particularly marked when seen from the side, e.g. walking. Unlike the side view, the frontal view reveals comparatively little of the interplay of motion, because our eyes cannot fully appreciate the swing of the arms and the stride of the legs. The same applies to sitting, kneeling and bending down. Most figures can therefore be given their characteristic form if the wood is cut out in side view.

The metal lay figure shown here is designed for creating this view so that a pattern can be made from it. It represents the most important charac-

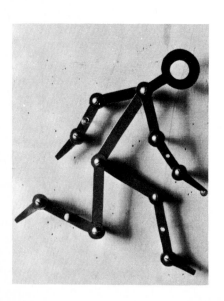

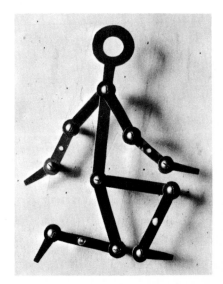

teristic positions of the limbs, moving straight to the front and the rear. In time, and with practise, your powers of imagination will become further developed, and you will be able to include additional lateral movements in your drawing.

The supple lay figure shows clearly how easy it is to represent movement if you begin with a simple framework of lines instead of immediately trying to tackle the intricate natural (or even abstract) representation of the body.

As we have already mentioned, all you have to do is consider what movements are possible.

Do not trace the lay figure with a pencil: freely sketch the fixed movements or positions. The lay figure is a simple teaching aid meant to help you with your designs; with it you can represent figures jumping, kneeling, crawling, sitting, walking, etc. By playing with it you will discover many other forms of movement which will inspire new ideas and designs.

Using the lay figure for carving

(1) The figure is positioned to represent a shepherd resting on his staff.
(2) The hands are imagined gripping the staff, and the skeleton clothed with generous outlines.
(3) The body is dressed and a hat, hair and beard put on the head.

(4 and 5) The outline now forms the pattern for the figure block, which can be marked and cut out.

How to make a simple lay figure

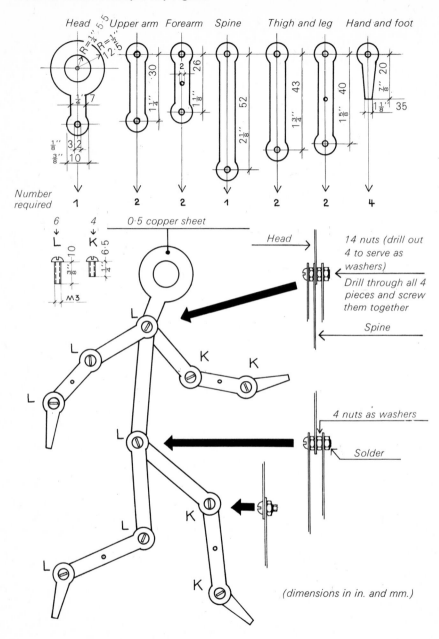

Head   Upper arm   Forearm   Spine   Thigh and leg   Hand and foot

$R=1\frac{3}{4}''$ 5.5
$R=\frac{1}{2}''$ 12.5

$\frac{1}{4}''$ 7

$\frac{1}{8}''$ 3.2
$\frac{3}{8}''$ 10

30   $1\frac{1}{4}''$

2
26   $1\frac{1}{8}''$

52   $2\frac{1}{8}''$

43   $1\frac{3}{4}''$

40   $1\frac{5}{8}''$

20   $\frac{7}{8}''$
35   $1\frac{1}{8}''$

Number required   1   2   2   1   2   2   4

6   4   0·5 copper sheet

L   K

L   10 $\frac{3}{8}''$ K   6.5 $\frac{1}{4}''$

M3

Head →

L

L

L   K   K

L

14 nuts (drill out 4 to serve as washers)

Drill through all 4 pieces and screw them together

Spine

L   K

K

4 nuts as washers

Solder

L

K

L

K

(dimensions in in. and mm.)

64

Methods of carving
individual features

You are now in a position to work out a systematic approach to your carving, which can be adapted as necessary to individual instances. Almost everything can be traced systematically. Individual carvers may proceed very differently when they carve a face, for instance; nevertheless, each of them will have become used to a certain method. Even if this is strongly personal, it can always be broken down into details and thus stored for use when required.

This does not mean that the experienced wood carver, once he has become accustomed to a certain method, uses only this and no other to achieve his aim. On the contrary, he rings the changes on several versions according to their suitability for what he happens to have in mind at the moment.

The following pages contain only basic directions: how can one carve a face, an eye, a nose, and so on?

The numbers indicate the sequence of the operations.

Carving a simple face

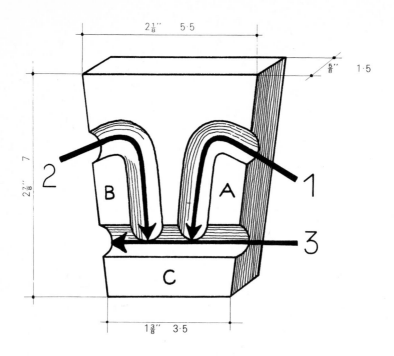

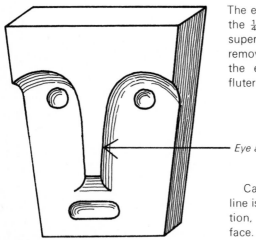

The eye and nose ridge is carved with the $\frac{1}{4}$ in. or 7 mm. fluter (A $\frac{1}{4}$). The superfluous material A, B and C is removed with shallow gouge B $\frac{5}{8}$, and the eyes and mouth gouged with fluter A $\frac{1}{4}$.

Eye and nose ridge

Carving the eye and nose ridge or line is the most important basic operation, since it immediately creates a face.

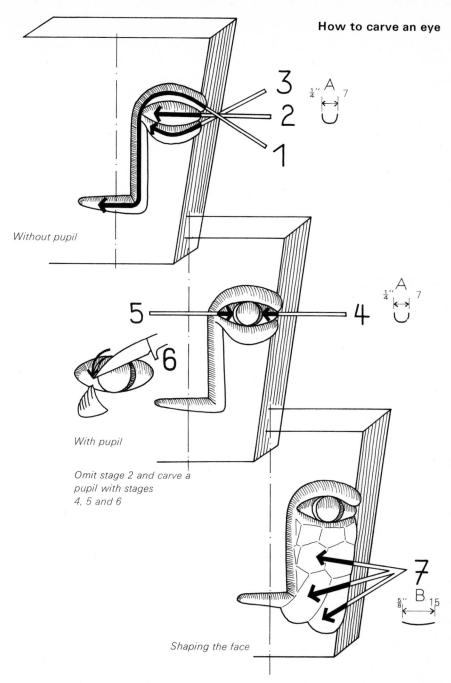

How to carve an eye

Without pupil

With pupil

Omit stage 2 and carve a
pupil with stages
4, 5 and 6

Shaping the face

Masks

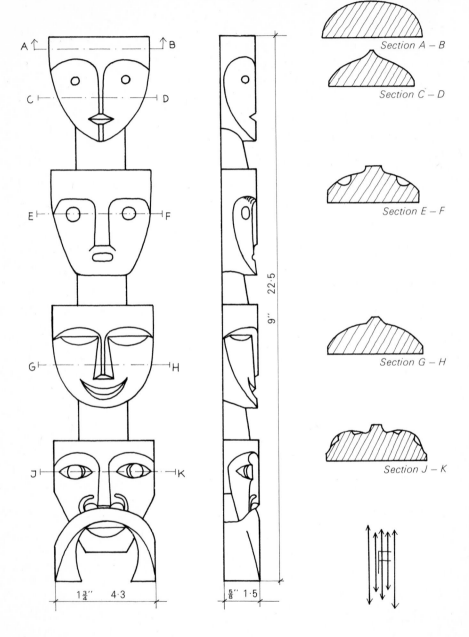

Section A – B

Section C – D

Section E – F

Section G – H

Section J – K

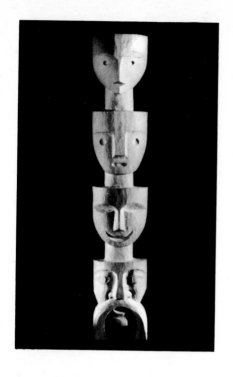

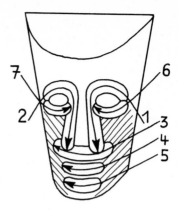

mouth and chin are indicated by seven grooves, deeply cut with fluter A $\frac{1}{4}$. The hatched areas indicate the ridges of material produced on the face.

Developing the face

Start with a block of wood which is convex at the front. The eyes, nose,

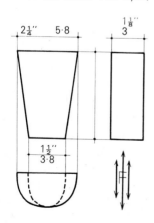

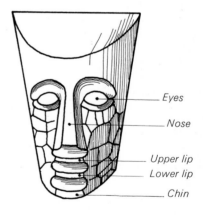

— Eyes

— Nose

— Upper lip
— Lower lip

— Chin

The ridges are now carved away to the depth of the grooves, leaving eyes, nose, mouth and chin projecting from the face. The shallow gouge B $\frac{5}{8}$ is used for this stage.

Noses

So far the nose has not projected from the carved face. This can be changed if the profile of the face is designed first and the forehead and mouth parts reduced.

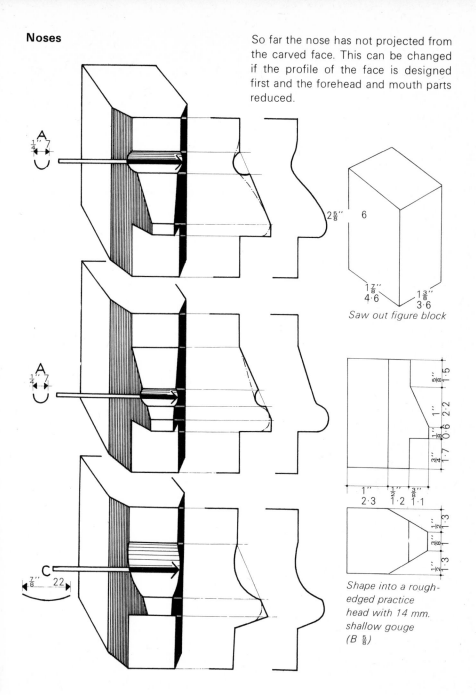

Saw out figure block

Shape into a rough-edged practice head with 14 mm. shallow gouge (B $\frac{5}{8}$)

A face with strong features

The main carved edges are clearly shown in the photograph (see opposite page). They impart an austere expression to the face.

The figure block is tapered on one narrow side. This eliminates the danger of carving a flat face from the beginning. In the drawings on the following pages each working stage is indicated by finely hatched cut planes and boldly cut edges. You will quickly understand the method of carving the edges if you consult both the drawings and the photograph repeatedly.

The face tapers towards the front. Aspect F shows the face frontally at all working stages, aspect P the profile.

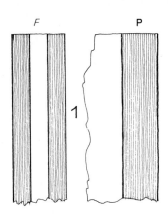

Bring out the forehead (a) and the ridge of the nose (b) by cutting back the tapered face area. The shallow gouge B $\frac{5}{8}$ or the carving knife is used for this purpose.

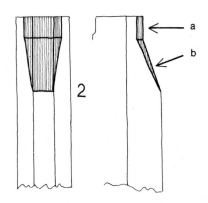

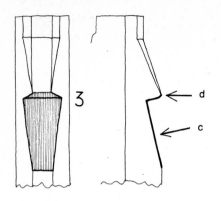

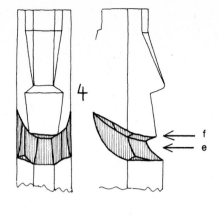

Now mark the end of the nose by a deep incision, slightly downwards. Chip away in the opposite direction to form the mouth and chin area (c). The tip of the nose (d) can now be seen in profile. Here the shallow gouge only should be used.

Develop the throat (e) by cutting a recess with the carving knife. This forms the lower end of the head and indicates the chin (f).

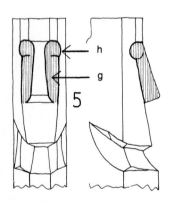

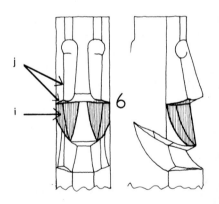

The nose is cut free so that it projects from the face (g). The upper transverse grooves form the eye sockets (h). Use fluter A $\frac{1}{4}$.

At this stage the mouth part is narrowed down with shallow gouge B $\frac{5}{8}$, so as to form the cheeks (i). A ridge of material (j) has been left towards the upper part of the face.

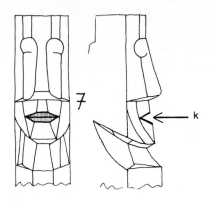

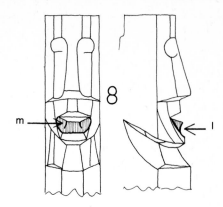

Now recess the mouth with the carving knife. In profile it will be clearly seen as a groove (k), while its frontal aspect will indicate whether the mouth portion has been tapered correctly.

The chin is now recessed (l) and at the same time the mouth is refined by lateral grooves towards the corners (m).

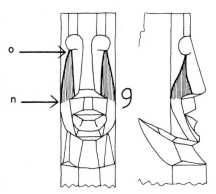

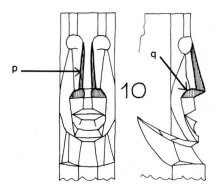

The carving away of the ridges of material left at stage 6 has the effect of tapering also the upper part of the face. It now merges without transition (n) with the cheeks. The cheek bones (o) are now formed with shallow gouge B $\frac{5}{8}$.

Chamfer the nose (p), making it narrower and finer. Correct the lateral areas below the nose with a slight upwards swing (q). Again the shallow gouge B $\frac{5}{8}$ helps at both stages.

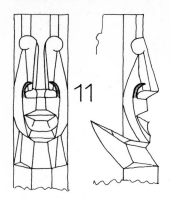

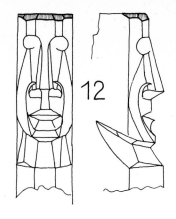

Produce the flare of the nostrils with two incisions cut with the veiner J $\frac{1}{16}$. If this tool is not available, simply use the carving knife or shallow gouge B $\frac{5}{8}$.

Finally, chamfer the crown of the head.

Reproducing different head positions

As if by magic compulsion, almost all beginners carve their heads in a straight position. As soon as a different position is required they will at once become very uncertain and lose all confidence.

The many operations involved in turning a natural, straight head in different directions may appear confusing at first. However the solution will at once become extremely simple if you rid yourself of the thought of an object with a wealth of detail.

To solve the problem, imagine a roughly-shaped head and reduce it in your mind to a simple cube. The final head is of no interest at the moment;

all you have to study now are its rotary movements, while the trunk remains stationary. Follow this through with a simple figure block and the drawings on the next two pages, after which any further explanation should be unnecessary.

Before you start carving, you can easily experiment with the positions shown in the explanatory sketches (from A 1 to E 2) using two blocks from a child's box of bricks.

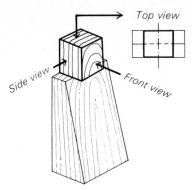

Figure block with practice head

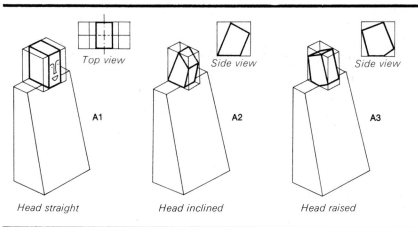

Top view

A1

Head straight

Side view

A2

Head inclined

Side view

A3

Head raised

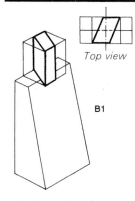

Top view

B1

Head turned to right

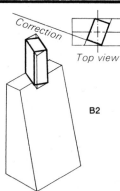

Correction

Top view

B2

The face is corrected by squaring off

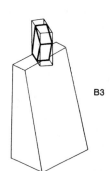

B3

This head can also be inclined (or raised)

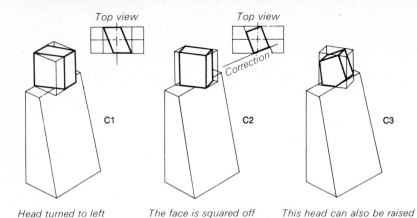

Top view

C1

C2

Correction

C3

Head turned to left

The face is squared off

This head can also be raised (or inclined)

Front view

D1

Correction

Front view

D2

E1

Front view

E2

Head tilted to right

The top is squared off

Head tilted to left

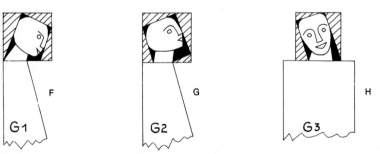

F

G1

G

G2

H

G3

The subsequent execution of the rounded shape of the head creates no further difficulties

The tilted head can also be inclined upwards or downwards

Hair

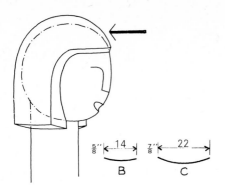

B   C

Depending on the hairstyle, a hood or suitable cap is left when the top of the head is carved; it is then converted into strands or locks of hair as required.

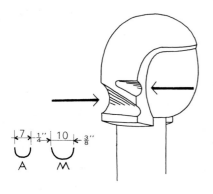

A   M

Waves can be carved with the gouge.

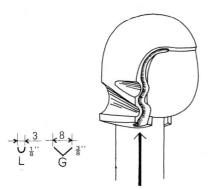

L   G

A long incision following the waves suggests a curling lock of hair.

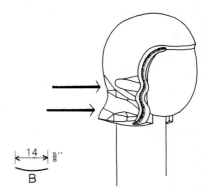

B

Sharp edges are chamfered with the shallow gouge. The hair is now ready for the texturing cuts.

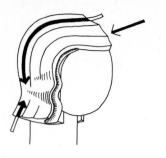

Carving the hair

Rough indication of the hair with the shallow gouge (note cut edges).

Rendering of the hair with the parting tool.

Rendering of the hair by closely-spaced gouge cuts.

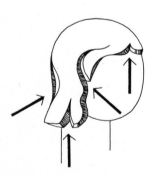

The hair can be 'fluffled out' by vigorous cuts along the edges with the parting tool.

The 'woodworm technique'

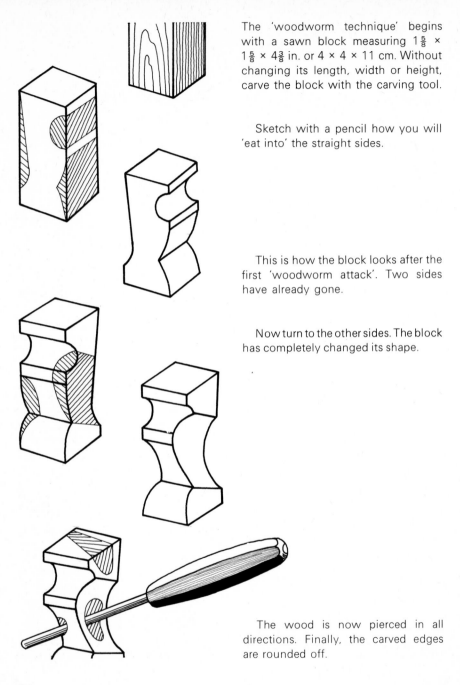

The 'woodworm technique' begins with a sawn block measuring $1\frac{5}{8}$ × $1\frac{5}{8}$ × $4\frac{3}{8}$ in. or 4 × 4 × 11 cm. Without changing its length, width or height, carve the block with the carving tool.

Sketch with a pencil how you will 'eat into' the straight sides.

This is how the block looks after the first 'woodworm attack'. Two sides have already gone.

Now turn to the other sides. The block has completely changed its shape.

The wood is now pierced in all directions. Finally, the carved edges are rounded off.

These examples of 'woodworm technique' were created by members of an
adult education class.

The transition to a particular shape

Several 'woodworm exercises' will give you more confidence in handling the carving tool and working with wood. The 'woodworm technique' does not aim at creating a particular shape. Its sole object is to carve the block at random as a means of practise. This makes the carver's hand bolder and leads to increasing appreciation of the possibilities of unfamiliar shapes.

For further practice, create a well-defined and intelligible figure again. Continue carving with complete abandon, but this time clearly imagining a certain shape. This enables you to test your own powers of imagination and expression. You may choose, for instance, the subject of a seated person.

Natural originals are confusing, because it is difficult to carve a body with anatomical correctness. However, if we lack the skill we may plead artistic licence, and all that is important in this nature-derived motif is that it should be clearly recognizable.

It is not difficult to imagine a simple figure sitting at ease. All parts of the body can be radically simplified or merely hinted at. What the head will look like, how long the neck is going to be — it does not matter whether the result is due to lack of ability, accident or deliberate effort. To begin with only the message of the sculpture is important. If you have succeeded in conveying this — no matter how grotesque it may look — the will to create a definite form has already won a victory over the material. This creative urge will undergo such strict training in the course of many such tasks that in time you will master all the finer sculptural details.

In the photographs on the opposite page, this progression to mastery of the material is clearly summarized. The first illustration shows once again an abstract 'woodworm' effort. After sufficient practise with such compositions you can return from the arbitrary to a deliberate rendering of a particular form. Set yourself simple tasks first, such as the seated figure already mentioned (2). Subject 3 (a child on its mother's lap) makes increased demands. Figure 4 shows a child sitting on the broad shoulders of a walking man. The walking stick provides a good support for the figure.

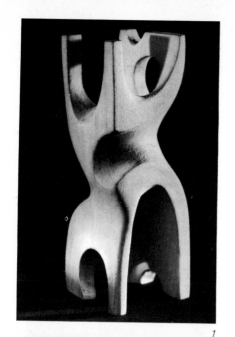

1

2

3

4

Chip carving

Chip carving, or flat carving, is the name given to the technique of carving signs, symbols and figures into the surface of the wood. It is eminently suitable for the adornment of signboards, furniture, doors and architectural items. Chip carvings offer many possibilities for artistic creation, and can be used to decorate a room much like paintings.

The basic form of chip carving is a simple incision in the wood. One of the oldest types, which remains popular even today, is the triangular cut (Fig. 1). The tools most frequently used for this are the carving knife and the straight and the skew chisel, or the shallow gouge; the fluter can be used for marking out (Fig. 1). The parting tool is also eminently suitable, as it removes the chip in one cut (Figs. 2 and 3).

But you need not confine yourself entirely to the triangular cut. The gouge produces the notch or thumbnail cut (Fig. 2), and the three-sided chisel the square cut (Fig. 3). The latter can also be made with the parting tool (Fig. B 1–3).

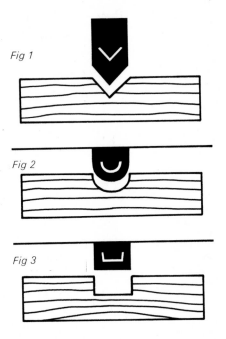

Fig 1

Fig 2

Fig 3

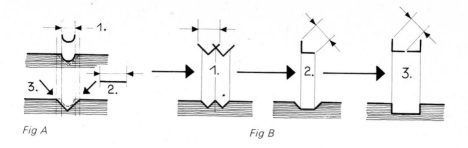

Fig A   Fig B

The triangular, notch and square cuts can be modified whenever required (Figs. 4–6). The cross-section need not always be uniform. Nor need a surface carving consists of only a single type of cut; there is no reason why all of them should not be used, as in Fig. 7.

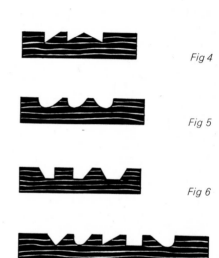

Fig 4

Fig 5

Fig 6

Fig 7

The 'Astronaut' shown on the next page provides a simple exercise for this technique. Very closely spaced and deep cuts should be avoided (Fig. 8). This not only looks ugly, but also makes carving needlessly difficult. Particularly in cuts across the grain, there is a risk of pieces of wood breaking off.

Fig 8

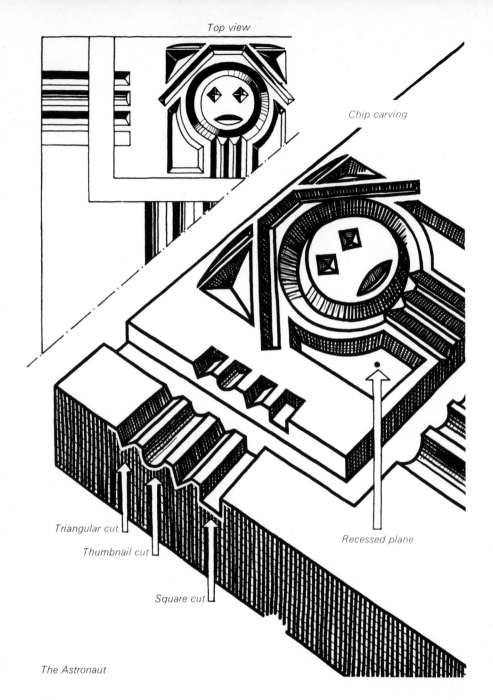

Top view

Chip carving

Recessed plane

Triangular cut

Thumbnail cut

Square cut

The Astronaut

1st exercise

These exercises are designed to familiarise you with the concept of low and high relief. They apply to the fields of chip carving, lettering and relief carving. The panels ($6\frac{3}{8}$ × 2 × $\frac{3}{4}$ in. or 16 × 5 × 1·8 cm.) are first decorated with triangular grooves ($\frac{1}{8}$ in. or 0·3 cm. deep). Precision — and therefore patience — are even more important here than in figure carving. Before you begin, ensure that the tools are sharp. This helps to avoid roughness and ensures that the chips come away cleanly. The cuts on the panels are first marked out with the fluter and finished with the chisel; this method ensures perfectly clean cuts. The recessed areas are carved with the shallow gouge. Carry out the same exercises with a perfectly sharpened parting tool.

2nd exercise

Try these wall decorations, then proceed to the two designs shown on the next page. The 'New City' shows a silhouette of towering skyscrapers. The austere rectangular shapes are enlivened by the windows. The design can be composed of several small panels. The 'Old City' is carved from a rectangular panel. Here gables, sloping roofs and spires dominate the picture; their vertical emphasis is counterbalanced by the transverse cuts of the sky.

89

The New City

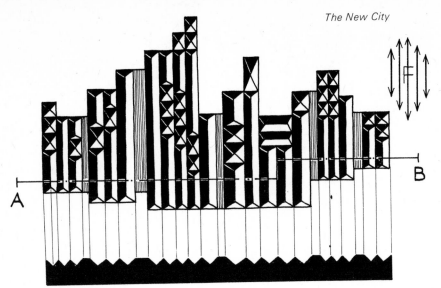

Dimensions: $7\frac{5}{8} \times 4 \times 1\frac{1}{8}$ in. or
18·9 × 10·2 × 3 cm.

Section A – B

The Old City

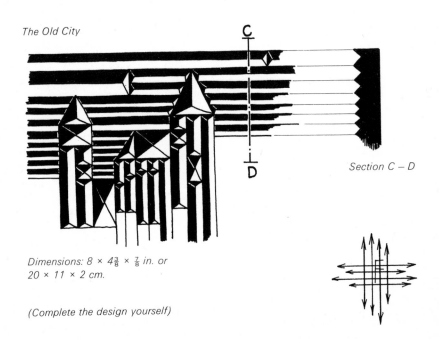

Dimensions: $8 \times 4\frac{3}{8} \times \frac{7}{8}$ in. or
20 × 11 × 2 cm.

(Complete the design yourself)

Section C – D

The expression of emotions in a chip-carved face

The human face can express many emotions — pleasure, grief, anger, indifference or fury. The corresponding facial expressions are produced by contraction or relaxation of the various features and can be recognised by the wrinkles and dimples which result. The mouth area is particularly important here. When you laugh the corners of your mouth are pulled upwards, when you are sad, downwards; in a dull, mask-like everyday expression the mouth remains static.

The clean cut of the carving tool is eminently suited to characterising the different human moods. So long as the expression is well defined, you should have no difficulty in representing it.

Carve faces expressing various moods into a narrow board, using a triangular cut.

For developments of these expressions see the two faces on the next page.

The first face shows a cheerful mood. Strong incisions represent the dimples caused by laughing. The up-turned corners of the large mouth are the most decisive feature.

The second face shows depression, expressed by the down-turned mouth and eyebrows.

For this exercise, the lines of each face should be traced on a planed board measuring $2\frac{1}{4} \times \frac{5}{8} \times 5\frac{3}{8}$ in. or $5 \cdot 7 \times 1 \cdot 5 \times 13 \cdot 5$ cm.

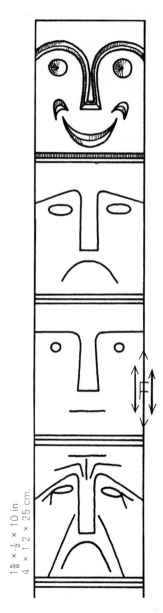

$1\frac{5}{8} \times \frac{1}{2} \times 10$ in.
$4 \times 1 \cdot 2 \times 25$ cm.

Chip-carved figures

Not everyone will find it in him to carve a figure in the round, and the chip-carved decoration of a figure block offers a simple but satisfying alternative. Whether the block is rounded off first, or merely cut out with a power saw, leaving all the edges square, is entirely up to you. A sawn-out figure abounding with rough edges and corners can be given just as much character as a rounded one, and if you enter the vast field of abstract representation there is no limit to what you can do.

The following photographs serve as examples of the possibilities in abstract woodcarving.

The titles of the illustrations are:

1. Affection
2. Embrace
3. Mammon
4. Hair-raising
5. Knitting needles
6. Arrogance

Decorating figures with triangular-cut ornaments should not present any difficulties; alternatively they can be merely painted with decorative patterns. In either case the surface of the figure should first be given a general tool finish or sandpapered. A couple of examples are shown in the following illustrations of the Cat and the Astronaut. The framed numbers indicate the sequence of sawing for the figure blocks.

1

2

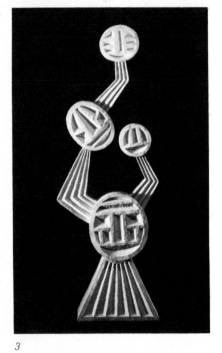

3

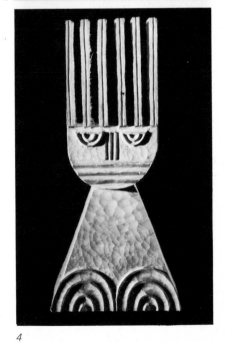

4

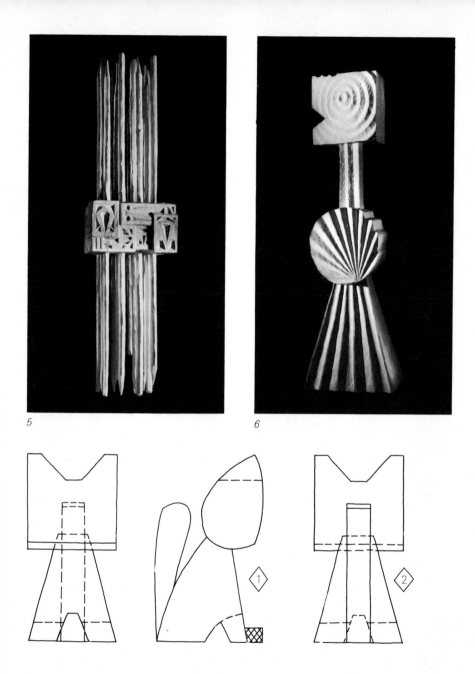

Cat: dimensions $1\frac{1}{4}$ × $1\frac{5}{8}$ × $3\frac{5}{8}$ *in. or 3·3 × 4 × 8·9 cm.*

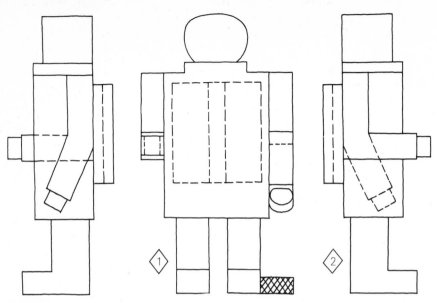

Astronaut: dimensions $2\frac{1}{4}$ × $1\frac{5}{8}$ × 4 in. or 5·7 × 4 × 10·2 cm.